Hi guys

First things first – thanks for buying this lovely little Comic Relief book! The £3 you've paid for it will be used to change lives, not only in Africa, but right here at home too.

And that's not all you can do to make a difference. The book starts off with three simple, delicious cake recipes – all you have to do is bake one (or all of them!), sell the cakes to your friends, family, colleagues or schoolmates and you'll have raised an extra few quid for Comic Relief and their brilliant causes. What could be easier?

You can make as many cakes as you like, simply by multiplying the quantities in the ingredients list. The more trays you bake, the more money you make! On the next two pages there are some tips on how to organize your sale from the people at Comic Relief. So get yourself baking, have some fun and raise loads of cash.

The cakes are not the only big treats in the book, though ... there are some fantastic recipes in there for you and your family to enjoy too.

So you're all set. And if you're still wondering whether you really should go to the trouble of organizing that cake sale, please remember that every single penny you raise counts.

Last year I was lucky enough to go and see some of the Red Nose Day money at work – at a children's centre for kids infected with HIV/AIDS in a township just outside Johannesburg. Every penny of Comic Relief cash that's spent there makes a huge difference. It provides these kids with vital food (the stew they rustled up from next to nothing was amazing, by the way!), it helps them with medicine, care and education and, perhaps most importantly of all, it helps to spread a little love.

That's why I wanted to make this book for Comic Relief. And that's why it's seriously cool that you've already helped by buying it.

Have a great Red Nose Day.

Big love

Jamie x

THE BIG COMIC RELIEF BAKE-UP

Here are three amazing cake recipes that are dead simple to make. They're full of proper ingredients like Fairtrade chocolate, organic eggs, dried fruits and healthy nuts and they taste fantastic to boot.

Perfect to flog to your mates at work or school!

You can bake as many trays as you like – just multiply the ingredients accordingly, depending on how big your cake sale or Red Nose Day party is going to be. Easy!

THE ULTIMATE CAKE SALE GUIDE

You've made your cakes and you're all set to sell – follow the Five Ps below and you'll raise potfuls of cash.

1. Plan – Get friends involved to help out ... whether it's cooking or selling, the more the merrier!

2. Promote your event – There are downloadable posters at www.rednoseday.com/jamie to help too.

3. Purchase – Buy the Big Red Nose at Sainsbury's and the coolest charity T-shirt the world has ever seen at T K Maxx and make your sale a real Comic Relief event.

4. Pay in – Don't forget to pay your money in! You can send it by cheque or postal order to Red Nose Day 2007, Ernst & Young, PO Box 51543, London SE1 2UG. For other ways to pay, go to www.rednoseday.com.

And number 5? Be PROUD. You've just done a very good thing indeed!

A LITTLE GOES A LONG WAY

The cash you raise will be used to help turn lives around in Africa and the UK. Here are just some of the ways you can make a difference.

In Africa

- £10 can pay for a medical kit to help a community carer look after those who are sick with HIV or AIDS.
- £25 can pay the school fees for a child living in extreme poverty in Ethiopia for a whole year.
- £100 can pay for a family in Tanzania to receive healthcare, food, education and counselling to help them care for a parent living with HIV or AIDS.

In the UK

- £10 can pay for food parcels and essential toiletry packs for a young homeless person.
- £20 can buy clothes and food for a mother and her children who have had to flee their home because of domestic violence.
- £50 can provide toys for a toy library in a poor and disadvantaged area so that parents can play with their children even when they can't afford to buy the toys themselves.

However much you manage to raise, you'll be making a BIG difference – thank you.

for Sale
I 07
RND
for Sale
for Sale
for sale

Fruity flapjacks

makes 16

4 tablespoons golden syrup
200g brown sugar
250g butter
350g oats
150g mixed dried fruit, like cherries, cranberries, apricots or prunes (chopped if necessary)
optional: 3 pieces of stem ginger, finely chopped

Preheat the oven to 150°C/300°F/gas 2. Lightly butter a 20 x 30cm (or similar sized), 4cm deep baking tray.

Put the syrup, sugar and butter into a large saucepan. Place on a medium heat until the butter has melted and everything is bubbling and caramel-coloured. Take the pan off the heat and stir in the oats, dried fruit and stem ginger, if using. Pour the mixture into the baking tray and press it down with the back of a wooden spoon to make it smooth and flat.

Bake in the preheated oven for 40 to 45 minutes. Leave to cool in the tin for 15 minutes before cutting into portions with a sharp knife. Don't take the individual flapjacks out of the tray yet, though; leave them until completely cool, then use a fish slice or spatula to get right down to the bottom of the tray and lift them out.

PS For Red Nose Day why not try decorating each of your fruity flapjacks with a glacé cherry!

Fairy cakes

makes 18

for the sponge

225g unsalted butter, softened, plus extra for greasing

225g caster sugar

4 large free-range or organic eggs

225g self-raising flour, sifted, plus extra for dusting

zest of 1 lemon

for the icing

150g icing sugar, sifted

18 strawberries, hulled, or other seasonal red fruit

Preheat the oven to 190°C/375°F/gas 5 and place 18 paper cases into muffin tins.

To make your sponge mixture, beat the butter and sugar together, using an electric whisk or by hand with a wooden spoon, until very light and fluffy. Add the eggs one at a time, beating each one in well before you add the next, then fold in the flour and lemon zest.

Spoon the mixture evenly into your muffin tins. Place in the preheated oven and bake for 15 minutes. You can check to see if the cakes are cooked by sticking a cocktail stick into the centre of one of them. Remove it after 5 seconds and if it comes out clean they're cooked; if it's slightly sticky they'll need a bit longer, so put them back into the oven for another 5 minutes, or until cooked through and golden on top. If you cook them for too long, though, they will go dry, so keep an eye on them. Remove the cakes from the tins and let them cool on a rack.

Now's the time to make your icing. Add a tablespoon of water at a time to the sifted icing sugar and stir. Keep adding water until you have a smooth paste – you'll need about 60ml of water altogether.

When the cakes have cooled, drizzle a teaspoon of your icing over each one and top with a strawberry or other seasonal red fruit.

for
sale

Bloomin' brilliant brownies

makes 20

250g unsalted butter
200g dark Fairtrade chocolate (70% cocoa solids), broken up
optional: 75g dried sour cherries
optional: 50g chopped nuts
80g cocoa powder, sifted
65g plain flour, sifted
1 teaspoon baking powder
360g caster sugar
4 large free-range or organic eggs
optional: 250ml crème fraîche
optional: zest of 1 orange

Preheat your oven to 180°C/350°F/gas 4. Line a 25cm square baking tray with greaseproof paper. In a large bowl over some simmering water, melt the butter and the chocolate and mix until smooth. Stir in the cherries and nuts, if you're using them. In a separate bowl, mix together the cocoa powder, flour, baking powder and sugar, and add this to the chocolate, cherry and nut mixture. Stir together well. Beat the eggs, add to the bowl, and stir until you have a silky consistency.

Pour your brownie mix into the baking tray and place in the oven for around 25 minutes. You don't want to overcook them, so, unlike cakes, when you test them with a skewer it shouldn't come out all clean. The brownies should be slightly springy on the outside but still gooey in the middle. Allow to cool in the tray, then carefully transfer to a large chopping board and cut into chunky squares. These make a fantastic dessert served with a dollop of crème fraîche mixed with some orange zest.

for Sale
for sale

THE RED NOSE CLASSIC COLLECTION . . .

We all want to make the world a better place. By buying this book and rustling up those lovely brownies, fairy cakes and flapjacks for your sale, you have made a fantastic contribution already. Now, with this next lot of recipes, you can make a difference in your own home. Get everyone involved, have a laugh in the kitchen, then sit down and enjoy the lovely food you've cooked – together.

Here is a selection of fun, tasty, simple recipes to get you going. Get stuck in!

The ultimate burger and chips

makes 8 burgers

1kg chuck steak, or good minced steak
1 onion, peeled and finely chopped
olive oil
a pinch of cumin seeds
1 tablespoon coriander seeds
sea salt and freshly ground black pepper
a handful of freshly grated Parmesan cheese
1 heaped tablespoon English mustard
1 large free-range or organic egg
115g breadcrumbs
8 burger buns

for the chips
2kg large potatoes, skins left on, cut into 1cm thick chips
olive oil
1 whole bulb of garlic
freshly ground black pepper
3 sprigs of fresh rosemary
zest of 1 lemon
85g sea salt

First, if you're using chuck steak to make your burgers, slice it up and pulse it in a food processor. Put the meat into a bowl. In a big frying pan, slowly cook the onion in a little olive oil for about 5 minutes, until softened but not coloured. Add the onion to the meat – it will give sweetness to the burger. Using a pestle and mortar, bash up the cumin and coriander seeds with a pinch of sea salt and freshly ground black pepper until fine and add to the meat. Add the Parmesan, mustard, egg and half the breadcrumbs and mix well. If the mixture is too sticky, add a few more breadcrumbs.

Lay some greaseproof paper on a tray or large plate and sprinkle over some of the remaining breadcrumbs. Shape the meat into 8 fat burgers and place these on top of the crumbs on the tray. Sprinkle more crumbs on top and press down gently. The burgers are better if they are chilled before cooking, so put them in the fridge for an hour or so.

Half an hour before you want to cook the burgers, preheat the oven to 230°C/450°F/gas 8 and put in a large flat baking tray. Parboil your chips (still with their skins on) for about 10 minutes in salted boiling water and drain in a colander. Heat some olive oil in a frying pan. Smash the garlic bulb up and chuck the cloves into the oil, then add the chips. Toss in the oil and season with freshly ground black pepper. Transfer the contents of the pan to the preheated tray and cook for 20 to 25 minutes, until the chips are crisp and golden. Now make your rosemary salt (the unused salt can be saved for months in an airtight jar). Remove the leaves from the rosemary and put them in a pestle and mortar with the lemon zest and salt. Bash up to make a green paste, adding more salt if the mixture is too wet. Push this paste through a sieve and keep to one side until you're ready to serve.

Take your burgers out of the fridge and fry them in a little oil on a medium to high heat for about 8 to 10 minutes, depending on the thickness of the burgers and how you like them, turning occasionally. Serve them in toasted burger buns, with tomato ketchup, and your fat chips sprinkled with some rosemary salt.

Chicken noodle stir-fry

serves 2

200g dried medium egg noodles
sea salt and freshly ground black pepper
vegetable oil
4 tablespoons unsalted cashew nuts
1 tablespoon icing sugar
2 chicken breasts, skin off, cut into little strips
a bunch of fresh coriander, leaves picked and stalks finely chopped
2 big cloves of garlic, peeled and thinly sliced
a thumb-sized piece of fresh ginger, peeled and thinly sliced
8 spring onions, trimmed and thinly sliced
a handful of bean sprouts
2 tablespoons soy sauce
1 tablespoon fish sauce
1 gem lettuce, leaves separated, washed and spun dry
optional: a few sprigs of watercress
1 fresh red chilli, deseeded and sliced, to serve
1 lime, cut into wedges, to serve

Cook the noodles in boiling salted water according to the packet instructions. Drain and refresh under cold water, then drain again, toss in a little oil and put to one side. Toss the cashew nuts with a tablespoon of water and the icing sugar. Drop them into a hot saucepan and cook, shaking and tossing constantly, until the nuts turn sticky, then golden. Tip on to a baking tray to cool, then chop them or bash them up in a pestle and mortar.

Heat a frying pan or wok that's big enough to hold all the ingredients. Season the chicken with salt and pepper and stir-fry in a little vegetable oil for 2 to 3 minutes until almost cooked. Add the coriander stalks, garlic and ginger and cook for a further minute. Add the spring onions and nearly all the bean sprouts and stir-fry for a few seconds, then add the cooked noodles and the coriander leaves. Keep stir-frying until the noodles are warmed through, then season with the soy and fish sauces and remove from the heat.

Serve in bowls, decorated with the rest of the bean sprouts, the gem leaves, watercress sprigs, if using, and the cashew nuts. Garnish with sliced chilli and lime wedges.

Spaghetti with sweet cherry tomatoes, marjoram and extra virgin olive oil

serves 4

500g dried spaghetti, spaghettini or linguine
sea salt and freshly ground black pepper
300–400g lovely ripe red and yellow cherry tomatoes
2 good handfuls of fresh marjoram or basil, leaves picked
extra virgin olive oil
1 clove of garlic, peeled and finely sliced
1 tablespoon white or red wine vinegar

Put your pasta into a large pan of salted boiling water and cook according to the packet instructions until al dente. While it's cooking, halve the tomatoes, put them into a large bowl and add your herbs, about 7 lugs of olive oil, the garlic and the vinegar. Season to taste, and scrunch with your hands to slightly mush the tomatoes. Put to one side until the pasta's ready. Drain the pasta, and while still steaming hot, mix well with the tomatoes, check the seasoning and serve. Easy peasy. Serve warm or even cold, as a salad for picnics.

Cheesy quesadillas with guacamole and minted sour cream

serves 4

4 handfuls of freshly grated cheese: Red Leicester and Cheddar work well
1 red pepper, deseeded and finely chopped
1–3 fresh red chillies, deseeded and sliced
2 bunches of spring onions, trimmed and sliced
2 handfuls of fresh coriander, chopped
sea salt and freshly ground black pepper
8 large flour tortillas

for the guacamole
2 ripe avocados
2 ripe tomatoes, halved
1 clove of garlic, peeled and sliced
4 pinches of ground cumin
juice of 2–3 limes, to taste
extra virgin olive oil
a small tub of sour cream
2 sprigs of fresh mint, leaves picked and chopped
juice of 1 lemon

First, mix the cheese, red pepper, chilli, half the spring onions and half the coriander in a large bowl. Season with a little salt and black pepper and divide evenly on to 4 tortillas. Place the other tortillas on top, press down a little and put to one side.

For the guacamole, put the avocados, tomatoes, garlic, cumin and the other half of the coriander and spring onions into a food processor and pulse to a smooth but chunky paste. Remove to a bowl, correct the seasoning with salt, pepper and lime juice to taste and loosen with a little good olive oil.

Next, make the minted sour cream, which is easy – just mix the sour cream with the mint and season to taste with salt, pepper and lemon juice for a good twang.

I like to cook my quesadillas one by one in a hot, dry, non-stick pan for around a minute or until golden on each side (you could have a couple of pans going).

Once cooked, slice them into quarters and serve with your side dips and a cold beer.

Lamb rogan josh

serves 4

an 8cm piece of fresh ginger, peeled and grated
8 cloves of garlic, peeled and chopped
1 teaspoon ground turmeric
4 tablespoons natural yoghurt
1 teaspoon crushed black peppercorns
1kg lamb shoulder, cut into big cubes
5 medium red onions, peeled and halved
2 red peppers, halved and deseeded
4 fresh red chillies, deseeded
1 tablespoon green cardamom pods
½ tablespoon whole cloves
1 stick of cinnamon
2 tablespoons coriander seeds
4 small dried red chillies
vegetable oil
2 teaspoons paprika
600g tinned chopped tomatoes
sea salt
optional: sliced fresh chilli, coconut flakes, chopped herbs, to serve

The night before: Mix your ginger and garlic together and put into a bowl that's big enough to fit all the cubed lamb in. Add the turmeric, yoghurt and black pepper to the bowl and mix together. Tip the lamb into the bowl and stir it around until it's well coated with the yoghurt and spices. Cover and leave overnight in the fridge to marinate.

The day of cooking: Preheat your oven to 170°C/325°F/gas 3. Chop your onions and peppers roughly and whiz them in a food processor with the fresh red chillies. Get yourself an ovenproof pan and put it on the hob. On a medium heat, toast the cardamom pods, cloves, cinnamon and coriander seeds until they go a shade darker in colour. Then put them into a pestle and mortar and grind up with the dried red chillies. Keep the pan on the heat and add a splash of vegetable oil. Add the whizzed onion, pepper and chilli paste from the food processor with the ground up spices and the paprika. Cook over a gentle heat for about 10 minutes. By now, lots of delicious curry smells will be coming out of the pot.

Add the tomatoes, marinated lamb and 300ml of water, and stir well. When the curry comes to the boil, add half a tablespoon of salt, cover tightly with a lid and place in your preheated oven. You can basically forget about it now; all the hard work is done. Just wait 2 hours and carefully take the pot out of the oven. Taste it, and if it needs salt, add a little. If it's too hot, add a little yoghurt to cool it down. You can garnish with extra fresh chilli, coconut and herbs. Serve with rice, your favourite Indian bread such as paratha, naan or chapati, and loads of cold beer – you're going to need it!

Parmesan fish fillets with avocado and cress salad

serves 1

2 tablespoons flour
sea salt and freshly ground black pepper
170g white fish fillets, skin removed
1 free-range or organic egg, beaten
55g freshly grated Parmesan cheese
olive oil
½ a fresh red chilli, deseeded and finely chopped
1 ripe avocado, peeled and sliced lengthways
1 punnet of cress
1 tablespoon extra virgin olive oil
juice of ½ a lemon

Get a frying pan really hot. Season the flour with salt and pepper. Dust the fish fillets with the seasoned flour, then dip into the egg and press into the grated Parmesan, making sure the fish is nicely covered. Add a little olive oil to the hot pan and fry the fish fillets for a couple of minutes on each side until golden brown. Throw in the chilli. Mix together the avocado and cress with the extra virgin olive oil and lemon juice, and put on to your plate with your fish fillets.

Meatballs with pasta

serves 4–6

olive oil
½ a small red onion, peeled and finely sliced
a small bunch of fresh basil, leaves picked and stalks finely chopped
2 x 400g tins of good-quality tomatoes
sea salt and freshly ground black pepper
8 good-quality pork sausages
500g dried spaghetti
optional: freshly grated Parmesan cheese, to serve

Heat a medium-sized saucepan and pour in a splash of olive oil. Add the onion and fry slowly for several minutes, until soft and golden brown. Throw in the basil stalks, then add the tomatoes. Season well with salt and black pepper and simmer gently for 15 minutes until reduced a bit.

With a sharp knife, slit the sausages at one end. Squeeze out a ball of sausagemeat and roll it into a meatball. You should get 3 small balls from each sausage and end up with 24 meatballs.

Heat a large, heavy-based frying pan and pour in a splash of olive oil. Fry the sausage balls until they are brown all over, then remove from the pan and pour away the excess fat. Pour the tomato sauce into the frying pan and add the meatballs. If the tomato sauce is quite thick and the meatballs are poking out of the top, add a splash of hot water to loosen it up. Simmer for 15 minutes.

Meanwhile, bring a pan of salted water to the boil, drop in the spaghetti and cook according to the packet instructions until al dente. Sprinkle the sauce with the basil leaves and serve with the drained pasta and lots of freshly grated Parmesan, if you like.

Scottish Pete's cheesy steak sandwich

serves 1

My mate Peter Begg is one of my best friends and a fantastic cook. He used to work in the circus when he was younger, where he ran a kind of roulette stall, and this kept him busy for a few months travelling round America. Apart from some of his colourful stories about the bearded lady and the tattooed man, I remember the passionate way he talked about the cheesy steak sandwiches. Apparently thousands of these sandwiches would be sold from stalls in this travelling circus.

It basically involves getting a long submarine or baguette type roll and heating it in the oven at 150°C/300°F/gas 2 for 5 minutes or so until it's just warmed through and not too crispy. Then get yourself a nice piece of rib eye, sirloin or rump steak – not too thick – and bash it out with your fist or a rolling pin to make it a little thinner and tenderize it. Season it with sea salt and freshly ground black pepper and lay it on a very hot griddle pan. Obviously you can cook it to your liking, but I do mine medium rare.

Once the steak is nicely seared on one side, turn it over and immediately grate Provolone cheese over the top so it melts from the heat of the steak and mixes with the juices. Once the other side is done, place it on a board, slice it up, and stuff it into your baguette or submarine roll with some wild rocket. Pour some of the steak juice over the bread, squeeze over some yellow American mustard and tuck in. Sliced onions also go really well with it, so if you have some they can be cooked next to the steak in the pan.

American pancakes

serves 4

3 large free-range or organic eggs
115g self-raising flour
140ml milk
a pinch of salt
2 handfuls of blueberries
a mixture of sliced kiwi, sliced banana and quartered strawberries, to serve
Greek yoghurt, to serve
honey, to serve

Separate the eggs, putting the whites into one bowl and the yolks into another. Stir the flour and milk into the yolks, mix to a smooth thick batter, and leave to rest for 30 minutes. When you're ready to go, whisk the whites with the salt until stiff and fold into the batter, then fold in your blueberries.

Heat a heavy non-stick pan on a medium heat. Pour a spoonful of batter into the pan and fry for a couple of minutes until it starts to look golden and firm. Flip over and continue frying until both sides are golden and the pancakes are hot all the way through. You can make the pancakes any size you want.

When they're all ready, serve with the rest of the fruit, some yoghurt and a drizzle of honey.

THE BIG ONE
RED NOSE DAY
16 MARCH 07

THANKS

A BIG thanks to all the people that made this little book possible – great stuff, guys! Thanks to Bobby Sebire, Suzanna de Jong, Pete Begg, Ginny Rolfe, Anna Jones and Georgie Socratous; to Tom Weldon, John Hamilton, Tiina Wastie, Keith Taylor and Annie Lee at Penguin; to Kevin Cahill, Michele Settle, Ann Hall, Vanessa Russo, Kate Conway and Mark Woods at Comic Relief; to Paul Rider for the amazing photography and to Emma Brown for her brilliant assistance; to David Loftus for the beautiful food shots; to Metro Imaging for letting us use their photo studio; to Direct Lighting for letting us use their equipment; to SHOOT Production and The Horseman; to Maria Comparetto for sorting out my hair and makeup; to Stora Enso for their huge contribution towards the paper these books are printed on; to Quantus Print & Display for printing the counterpacks; to Mohn Media in Germany for helping out massively with the production costs; and to Dot Gradations Ltd for donating the colour reproduction.

Penguin Books Ltd, 80 Strand, London WC2R 0RL, England
www.penguin.com

Published by Penguin Books 2007

Some of the recipes in this book were taken from Jamie's *Happy Days with the Naked Chef* and *Jamie's Dinners*, published by Michael Joseph/Penguin.

Printed in Germany by Mohn media

ISBN: 978-0-141-03146-0

Comic Relief, registered with the Charity Commission, no. 326568